SHORT WALKS PEAK DISTRICT

BAKEWELL AND THE WHITE PEAK

by Andrew McCloy

Upper Cressbrook Dale (Walk 3)

CONTENTS

Using this guide... 4
Route summary table 6
Map key 7
Introduction... 9
   Walking in the White Peak... 10
   Where to stay... 10
   Caring for our national park... 11

The walks
1. Taddington, Chelmorton and Flagg 13
2. Tideswell Dale and Litton Mill 19
3. Litton and Cressbrook Dale 23
4. Monsal Head tunnel and viaduct................................ 29
5. Sheldon and Magpie Mine 33
6. Monyash and upper Lathkill Dale 39
7. Lower Lathkill Dale and Bradford Dale...................... 45
8. Elton and Robin Hood's Stride 51
9. Bakewell and the Monsal Trail 57
10. Bakewell, Manners Wood and the River Wye.............. 63
11. Stanton Moor 69
12. Chatsworth Park and Edensor 75
13. Beeley and Hob Hurst's House..................................... 79
14. Baslow Edge and Curbar Edge 85
15. River Derwent and Calver Weir.................................... 91

Useful information.. 95

USING THIS GUIDE

Routes in this book

In this book you will find a selection of easy or moderate walks suitable for almost everyone, including casual walkers and families with children, or for when you only have a short time to fill. The routes have been carefully chosen to allow you to explore the area and its attractions. Most routes are circular or out-and-back, although some linear walks may be included that use public transport to get back to the start. Although there may be some climbs there is no challenging terrain, but do bear in mind that conditions can sometimes be wet or muddy underfoot. A route summary table is included on page 6 to help you choose the right walk.

Clothing and footwear

You won't need any special equipment to enjoy these walks. The weather in Britain can be changeable, so choose clothing suitable for the season and wear or carry a waterproof jacket. For footwear, comfortable walking boots or trainers with a good grip are best. A small rucksack for drinks, snacks and spare clothing is useful. See www.adventuresmart.uk.

Walk descriptions

At the beginning of each walk you'll find all the information you need:

- start/finish location, with a what3words address to help you find it
- parking and transport information, estimated walking time, total distance and climb
- details of public toilets available along the route and where you can get refreshments
- a summary of the key highlights of the walk and what you might see

Timings given are the time to complete the walk at a reasonable walking pace. Allow extra time for extended stops or if walking with children.

The route is described in clear, easy-to-follow directions, with each waypoint marked on an accompanying map extract. It's a good idea to read the whole of the route instructions before setting out, so that you know what to expect.

Maps, GPX files and what3words

Extracts from the OS® 1:25,000 map accompany each route. GPX files for all the walks in this book are available to download at www.cicerone.co.uk/1257/gpx.

What3words is a free smartphone app which identifies every 3m square of the globe with a unique three-word address, e.g. ///destiny.cafe.sonic. For more information see https://what3words.com/products/what3words-app.

USING THIS GUIDE

Walking with children

Even young children can be surprisingly strong walkers, but every family is different and you may need to adapt the timings given in this book to take that into account. Make sure you go at the pace of the slowest member and choose a walk with an exciting objective in mind, such as a cave, river, waterfall or picnic spot. Many of the walks can be shortened to suit – suggestions are included at the end of the route description.

Dogs

Sheep or cattle may be found grazing on a number of these walks. Keep dogs under control at all times so that they don't scare or disturb livestock or wildlife. Cattle, particularly cows with calves, may very occasionally pose a risk to walkers with dogs. If you ever feel threatened by cattle, you should let go of your dog's lead and let it run free.

Enjoying the countryside responsibly

Enjoy the countryside and treat it with respect to protect our natural environments. Stick to footpaths and take your litter home with you. When driving, slow down on rural roads and park considerately, or better still use public transport. For more details check out www.gov.uk/countryside-code.

The Countryside Code

Respect everyone
- be considerate to those living in, working in and enjoying the countryside
- leave gates and property as you find them
- do not block access to gateways or driveways when parking
- be nice, say hello, share the space
- follow local signs and keep to marked paths unless wider access is available

Protect the environment
- take your litter home – leave no trace of your visit
- do not light fires and only have BBQs where signs say you can
- always keep dogs under control and in sight
- dog poo – bag it and bin it – any public waste bin will do
- care for nature – do not cause damage or disturbance

Enjoy the outdoors
- check your route and local conditions
- plan your adventure – know what to expect and what you can do
- enjoy your visit, have fun, make a memory

ROUTE SUMMARY TABLE

WALK NAME	START POINT	TIME	DISTANCE
1. Taddington, Chelmorton and Flagg	Taddington village centre	3hr	10km (6¼ miles)
2. Tideswell Dale and Litton Mill	Tideswell Dale car park	1½hr	5km (3 miles)
3. Litton and Cressbrook Dale	Litton village centre	2½hr	7.5km (4¾ miles)
4. Monsal Head tunnel and viaduct	Monsal Head Hotel	1½hr	5km (3 miles)
5. Sheldon and Magpie Mine	Sheldon village centre	1¼hr	4.5km (2¾ miles)
6. Monyash and upper Lathkill Dale	Monyash village centre	2¼hr	6.5km (4 miles)
7. Lower Lathkill Dale and Bradford Dale	Coldwell End car park, Youlgrave	3hr	9.5km (6 miles)
8. Elton and Robin Hood's Stride	Elton Church	1½hr	5km (3 miles)
9. Bakewell and the Monsal Trail	Bakewell Visitor Centre	1¾hr	6km (3¾ miles)
10. Bakewell, Manners Wood and the River Wye	Bakewell Visitor Centre	2¾hr	9km (5½ miles)
11. Stanton Moor	Birchover Quarry car park	1hr	4km (2½ miles)
12. Chatsworth Park and Edensor	Calton Lees car park, Chatsworth	2hr	6.5km (4 miles)
13. Beeley and Hob Hurst's House	Beeley village centre	2½hr	8km (5 miles)
14. Baslow Edge and Curbar Edge	Curbar Gap car park	2¼hr	7km (4¼ miles)
15. River Derwent and Calver Weir	Calver Bridge	1¼hr	4.5km (2¾ miles)

ROUTE SUMMARY TABLE

HIGHLIGHTS
Unspoilt villages, open fields, views
Wildflowers, peaceful waterside, old mill
Dramatic and nature-rich limestone valley
Railway heritage, tunnel and viaduct
Historic lead mining remains
Geology, caves, vanishing rivers
Dales, rivers, local customs, wildlife
Rocky tor, standing stones, hermit's cave
Scenic flat trail, riverside, town views
Woods and riverbank flowers, wildlife
Birch and heather moorland, stone circle, views
Landscaped park, stately home, estate village
Neolithic remains, heather moors
Sweeping views, open moorland, rocky outcrops
Wide tree-lined river, old mill and bridges, historic weir

SYMBOLS USED ON ROUTE MAPS

- **(S)** Start point
- **(F)** Finish point
- **(SF)** Start and finish at the same place
- **4→** Waypoint
- **~** Route line

MAPPING IS SHOWN AT A SCALE OF 1:25,000

0 KM 0.25 0.5
0 miles 0.25

DOWNLOAD THE GPX FILES FOR FREE AT
www.cicerone.co.uk/1257/gpx

Chatsworth House beside the River Derwent (Walk 12)

INTRODUCTION

Lathkill Dale (Walk 6)

It would be hard to imagine a more perfect setting for a series of short scenic walks than the limestone dales of the central and southern Peak District, often known as the White Peak. The landscape is a palette of soft greens and warm yellows, with an irregular patchwork of fields and woodland, tucked-away valleys and picture-postcard villages; but it is also undulating and occasionally dramatic, providing a great variety of walks that offer both gentle relaxation and also adventure and discovery in equal measure.

The White Peak is so called because of the limestone underpinning it, a pale or pearly white rock that you see above surface in the area's distinctive field walls, barns and many traditional village buildings. It gives the rolling countryside a bright feel, certainly compared to the sombre greys and earthy browns of the gritstone that is the dominant rock in the higher northern Peak District (often known as the Dark Peak).

The variety of habitats in the White Peak range from tree-lined rivers like the Wye and Derwent to purple heather moorland on the eastern edge. There are upland meadows interspersed with narrow valleys, like Lathkill Dale and Cressbrook Dale, where rocky crags, caves and screes lead down to fast-flowing streams. In turn, this supports a variety of wildlife, including brown hares, dippers, butterflies and skylarks. In late spring and early summer, many dales are awash with colourful wildflowers, including cowslips, mountain pansy, orchids and wild thyme.

This is a peopled landscape, too, settled for over a thousand years, with distinctive and deep-rooted village communities like Youlgrave, Taddington and Tideswell, where a family-run pub or cafe provides a perfect end to a walk. Few people are now involved in mining, but farming is still an important way of life; and look out for traditional local customs and festivals like well dressing.

Walking in the White Peak

The routes in this book explore many of the main villages and embrace the finest dales, including Monsal, Wye, Lathkill, Cressbrook and Bradford. Wander alongside gurgling streams or stride over springy heather moorland, while huge canopies of beech and oak offer shady woodland walks. Explore up close the White Peak's distinctive limestone geology, walk in the footsteps of lead miners or step out in style through the stately parkland of Chatsworth. All of the walks are circular or there-and-back, and most are accessible by public transport.

Most walks in this book involve some up and down – this is the Peak District, after all – and there are some with longer or steeper climbs, but the extra effort is usually repaid with spectacular views. Gentler options make use of a former railway line via Bakewell that is now a scenic walking/cycling trail through the hills; and there are also easier routes that follow riverbanks and valley-bottom paths.

Where to stay

At the heart of the White Peak is Bakewell, the area's only proper town. It's a popular tourist destination with countless cafes and, of course, the ubiquitous Bakewell Pudding, but despite the summer crowds there's an attractive historic core and a thriving livestock market. The Old House Museum near the church is a particular treasure trove when it comes to learning about the town's history.

Bakewell is just the right size to explore on foot and is the ideal base from where to set out on your White Peak walks. Local bus services radiate out from Bakewell to the villages,

The Magpie Mine site is open to the public (Walk 5)

Monsal Head viaduct (Walk 4)

Rutland Square, Bakewell (Walks 9 and 10)

as well as further afield to Buxton, Sheffield and Derby. The town also has several outdoor clothing and equipment stores, which is handy in case you've forgotten to bring your favourite sunhat.

There's a mix of accommodation across the White Peak, especially small campsites, youth hostels and self-catering options, with more choice around the fringes in centres like Matlock, Buxton and Chesterfield.

Caring for our national park

Bakewell is the headquarters of the Peak District National Park, the oldest national park in Britain, covering 1438km^2 (555 sq miles) across several counties. Since its founding in 1951 it has been a firm favourite with walkers, but you don't have to walk far to get away from the crowds and enjoy peace and quiet.

Indeed, exploring on foot is not just one of the most rewarding ways to discover the Peak District, it's also the most sustainable. The national park is a precious but fragile environment, where there's a delicate balance between recreation, conservation and the day-to-day life of farming communities, so enjoy this glorious landscape – but tread lightly.

Make sure to call into the National Park Visitor Centre in Bakewell to learn more and get help with your visit; and to put something back please support the work of the Peak District National Park Foundation, a charity set up to raise funds to care for the national park (www.peakdistrictfoundation.org.uk).

St Michael & All Angels Church, Taddington

WALK 1
Taddington, Chelmorton and Flagg

Start/finish	St Michael & All Angels Church, Main Street, Taddington
Locate	///wager.daredevil.anyway
Cafes/pubs	Pub in Taddington
Transport	Buses from Bakewell and Buxton
Parking	Roadside on Main Street, Taddington (SK17 9TU)
Toilets	No public toilets on route

Time 3hr
Distance 10km (6¼ miles)
Climb 215m

A fairly long but uncomplicated walk with far reaching views, crossing open fields to link three historic villages

This route across the open and peaceful limestone plateau west of Bakewell begins with a short pull out of Taddington, but after that it's fairly level and easy walking with expansive views. Taddington and Chelmorton are two of the highest villages in Derbyshire, and this walk weaves its way across a beautiful patchwork quilt of small fields separated by stone walls and frequent stiles.

Taddington village sits a height of over 340m

Distances from Taddington to Bakewell and London

1 From the church gate walk up Main Street to the road junction and turn left into Humphrey Gate, then immediately right on a narrow public footpath between buildings. Follow this up the hillside and across a lane to continue up towards **Sough Top**.

2 Go to the left of the hilltop mast and head west through a succession of level fields, keeping close to the wall on your right. Cross a lane and at a second road take a path across a wide strip of bumpy ground opposite that eventually drops down to **Chelmorton**.

At over 365m above sea level, the parish church of St John in Chelmorton is reputedly the highest church with a spire anywhere in England. Rather unusually, it is topped by a golden weathervane in the shape of a locust.

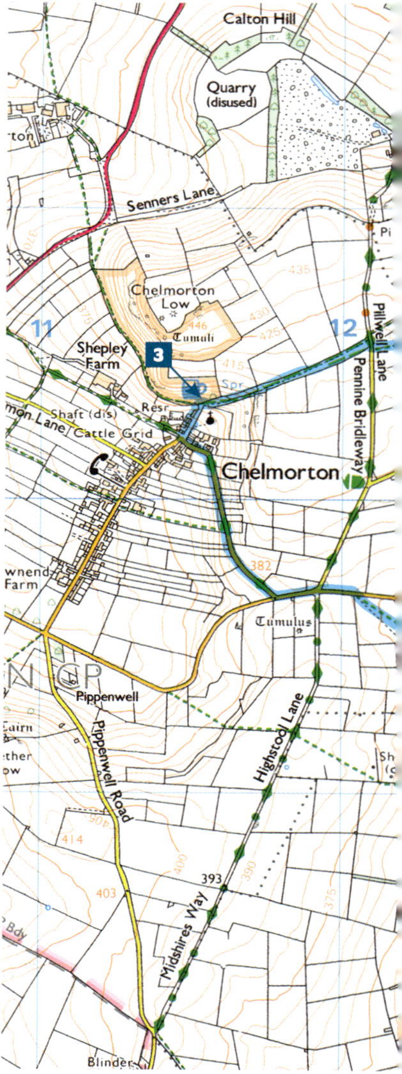

WALK 1 – TADDINGTON, CHELMORTON AND FLAGG

Chelmorton's village pub

3 Walk down the street past the church and pub and turn left into Church Lane. At the junction at the top go left and 200m beyond the next junction take the field path on the right. This drops down through a shallow valley and onwards to reach the edge of **Flagg** at High Stool Farm.

4 Cross the lane at the bend in front of you and continue in the same direction over more fields. The path eventually veers across to the left towards Flagg's main street. Join this and turn right down to the junction by the **chapel**. The Primitive Methodist Chapel was built in 1883 and its former Sunday School building next door is today a popular nursery school.

5 At the junction turn left on a path to the left of Flagg Hall and its farm sheds. With a wall on the right, follow this to the end of the path. Turn right into **Flagg Lane** and left just before Rockfield House. Follow field paths gently uphill for 200m, then go through a small gate in the wall on the right. The path continues diagonally left up through more fields to emerge at a road at the very top.

In this high, dry limestone country, Taddington once relied for drinking water on wells dug into its northern slopes, still marked on the map, while Chelmorton turned to a spring that fed a stream called Illy Willy Water.

WALK 1 — TADDINGTON, CHELMORTON AND FLAGG

> ⓘ There are 41,843km (26,000 miles) of drystone wall in the Peak District, which is more than the circumference of the Earth.

6 Turn left onto the road, with Taddington High Mere across to the right. This was where packhorses and livestock were once watered, but following restoration it's now a magnet for wildlife including newts and dragonflies. After 100m go right on a well-used sunken path that drops down to **Taddington**. Turn left to walk back along the village's main street to the start.

The historic walled fields of the White Peak

Narrow strip fields around Chelmorton

The White Peak is predominantly a livestock-rearing area, where sheep and cows are kept in open fields separated by drystone walls made from local limestone. They're 'dry' because traditionally no mortar is used and although skilfully made and generally robust, they do need patching up every now and then. Chelmorton still retains a distinctive rectangular field system that dates from late medieval times when each villager would have their own strip to farm. Look down from Church Lane and see how the narrow fields run at right angles from both sides of the village's main street.

Tideswell Dale

WALK 2
Tideswell Dale and Litton Mill

Start/finish	Tideswell Dale car park
Locate	///text.wisdom.comedy
Cafes/pubs	Cafes and pubs in Tideswell, cafe at Miller's Dale station on longer walk
Transport	Buses from Buxton
Parking	Tideswell Dale car park (SK17 8SN)
Toilets	At Tideswell Dale car park

Tucked away from the road, Tideswell Dale is a miniature haven for flowers and wildlife, with an easy valley-bottom path leading down to the larger Wye valley. Beyond is the peaceful hamlet of Litton Mill, dominated by its 18th-century former cotton mill. The return to Tideswell Dale is via a leafy stretch of the Monsal Trail, followed by a stepped but fairly steep descent down to cross the river.

Time 1½hr
Distance 5km (3 miles)
Climb 80m

A short outing via leafy Tideswell Dale to the historic Litton Mill, then back via the Monsal Trail

Riverside cottages at Litton Mill

SHORT WALKS PEAK DISTRICT

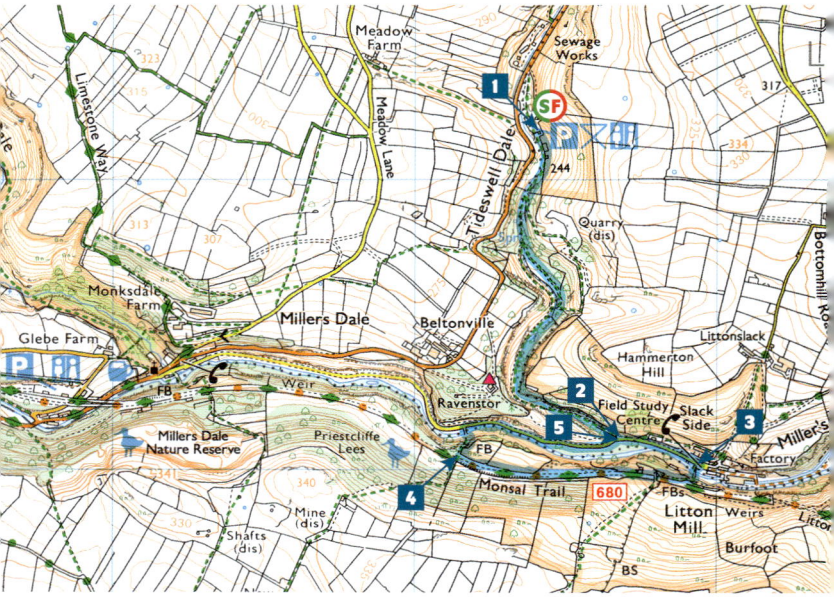

1 From the car park follow the obvious semi-surfaced path past the toilets and down **Tideswell Dale** beside the stream. A path on the left leads up to a disused quarry where basalt was once extracted for use in roadbuilding. Ignore a small footbridge on the right but go over a second footbridge and continue gently downhill through the increasingly tree-covered dale until after 1.5km you reach a minor road.

From April onwards the open lower slopes of the dale are carpeted by the unmistakable upright spikes of early purple orchids, while in summer look out for the pretty magenta flowers of bloody cranesbill, a type of wild geranium.

2 Turn left and walk along this quiet no through road until you reach the buildings of **Litton Mill**. Just before you get to the former mill itself, which you can walk up to but is now a private property with no public access, turn right on a narrow, signposted path between buildings, next to Riverside House.

WALK 2 – TIDESWELL DALE AND LITTON MILL

Litton Mill used powerful water wheels to harness the River Wye and operate textile machinery. This comparatively short river has over 25 mill sites, including others at Cressbrook and Bakewell, as well as much earlier corn mills.

3 At the end of the path go across a long footbridge, up a very short but rocky path, and at the top join the **Monsal Trail**. Turn right and walk along the former railway line for 700m until you reach a junction of routes. The path to the left leads into Derbyshire Wildlife Trust's Priestcliffe Lees Nature Reserve, a steep hillside renowned for its limestone-loving wildflowers.

4 Turn right, signposted **Ravenstor**, and follow this path down the steep hillside via a long flight of stone steps until you reach the River Wye, which you cross via another footbridge.

The ornate stone gateposts on your left mark a former entrance to Ravenstor, a large country house that you may have already glimpsed from the Monsal Trail. Since 1938 it has been a youth hostel.

Path junction in Tideswell Dale

Footbridge over the River Wye

Turn right and walk along the lane until you reach a small car park and the path into Tideswell Dale.

5 Turn left and follow the outward route back to the start.

(i) *The Peak District National Park is home to 38,000 people but visited by over 13 million every year.*

+ To lengthen
At Waypoint 4 continue along the easy, flat trail for nearly 1.5km to reach the former station at Miller's Dale, where there is a cafe and toilets, returning the same way for a round trip of around 1hr.

Litton Mill

Litton Mill was built in the 1780s to manufacture textiles. Although never particularly profitable, the mill was still operational until as recently as 1986, when it finally closed and was converted into residential apartments. Early on it gained a notoriety for

The former Litton Mill

its harsh working practices. The buildings around the mill were built for its workers and apprentices, and one young man, who spent a decade at the mill, described how he was poorly fed and badly treated, forced to work long hours in terrible conditions. His memoirs were serialised and used by campaigners protesting against the 'factory' system.

WALK 3
Litton and Cressbrook Dale

Start/finish	Litton village centre
Locate	///breakfast.central.butternut
Cafes/pubs	Pub and village shop (light refreshments) in Litton
Transport	Buses from Bakewell and Buxton
Parking	Roadside in Litton village centre (SK17 8QP)
Toilets	No public toilets on route

Time 2½hr
Distance 7.5km (4¾ miles)
Climb 185m

Explore a dramatic and nature-rich limestone valley from top to bottom on this adventurous route

Cressbrook Dale is an exceptional nature reserve boasting plunging semi-ancient woodland, a gurgling stream and steep grassy slopes topped with cliffs, scree and rocky pinnacles. This enjoyable and energetic walk involves steps, slopes and rough open hillside, going into the dale via a wooded hillside and valley-bottom path and back out along the high grassy rim with tremendous views.

Cressbrook Dale

23

SHORT WALKS PEAK DISTRICT

Litton shop in the former village smithy

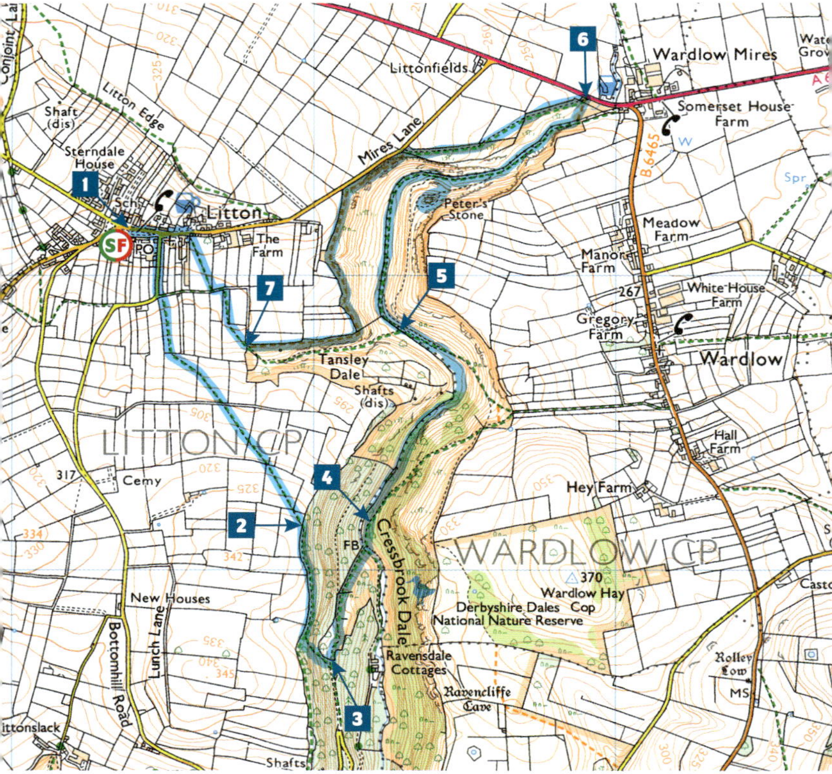

1 With your back to Litton Shop turn right and right again down a lane signposted Cressbrook. At the first bend take the footpath ahead down a long field. Swing half left in the next field and continue through several more to reach the top edge of **Cressbrook Dale**.

WALK 3 – LITTON AND CRESSBROOK DALE

On the far side of the valley the steep wooded slopes are topped by sheer cliffs where ravens and peregrine falcons nest. They include the appropriately named Ravenscliffe Cave, where remains have been found dating back to the Bronze Age.

2 Follow the path along the woodland edge, then turn left on a stepped path down the wooded hillside to reach a broad track at the bottom.

3 Turn left along the track, go through a gate, and out along the open dale on a clear path. Drop down steps and where you meet another path go left, across a footbridge, and along the bottom of the dale until you reach a fork. Mosses, lichens and ferns abound on trees and walls in the cool damp conditions beside the stream.

4 Take the left (lower) path at the fork and continue along the wooded path beside the stream. Emerge into the open and follow the path along the grassy bottom through **Cressbrook Dale National Nature Reserve** all the way until you reach a small plank bridge.

5 Don't cross the bridge but go straight on along the dale-bottom path. As it bends to the right make a short detour up the open slope to

Scree in Cressbrook Dale

Peter's Stone and upper Cressbrook Dale

inspect the limestone outcrop of **Peter's Stone**. The dale becomes shallower and at the very top, 150m before you reach the road at **Wardlow Mires**, veer left through a wall gap and across open ground to reach a gate.

> In 1815 Peter's Stone was the site of the last 'gibbeting' in Derbyshire, when the body of a Tideswell man was hung here after being executed for murder. The rock supposedly gets its name from its similarity to St Peter's Basilica in Rome!

6 Don't go through the gate to the road but instead turn hard left for a path along the inside edge of the wall. Walk across a field and then along the top edge of the dale with stunning views. Stay on this clear high-level route for 500m, eventually swinging right into **Tansley Dale** to join the

> ⓘ *The limestone underpinning the White Peak was formed 20 million years ago from deposits on the bed of what was then a warm tropical lagoon.*

WALK 3 – LITTON AND CRESSBROOK DALE

main path at the end. The bumps and hollows in Tansley Dale date from several centuries ago when miners from Litton dug for lead ore.

7 Go up across a field and turn left into a walled lane, then immediately right across another field to re-enter **Litton**. Turn left along the road back to the start.

> **– To shorten**
>
> At Waypoint 5 cross the simple bridge and follow the path ahead through Tansley Dale and a direct route back to Litton, saving just over 2km (around 45min).

The special nature reserves of Derbyshire Dales

Like Lathkill Dale (Walks 8 and 9), Cressbrook Dale is part of Derbyshire Dales National Nature Reserve designated for its rich limestone habitat. Cowslips, mountain pansies and spring sandwort dot the grassland and open slopes, while wheatears and redstarts flit between the scrub and lush mixed woodland, which includes ash, oak, elm and lime. From April onwards look out for the Green Hairstreak (Britain's only green butterfly) and the unmistakable Common Blue butterfly feeding on nectar-rich orchids.

Cressbrook Dale, part of Derbyshire Dales National Nature Reserve

Looking down on Monsal Head viaduct

WALK 4
Monsal Head tunnel and viaduct

Time 1½hr
Distance 5km (3 miles)
Climb 100m

A fairly easy but exciting short walk that goes both underground and up high to explore a Peak District beauty spot

Start/finish	*Monsal Head Hotel*
Locate	*///cooking.originate.bankwagon*
Cafes/pubs	*Pub and cafe at Monsal Head, pub at Little Longstone*
Transport	*Buses from Bakewell*
Parking	*Monsal Head car park (DE45 1NL)*
Toilets	*At Monsal Head car park*

You don't have to be a train buff to enjoy this short but dramatic walk along the former railway line turned recreational trail at Monsal Head. From the cool, dark depths of a tunnel you switch immediately to the airy heights of a viaduct, then descend to the picturesque river winding through the dale far below. This is a relatively easy walk with modest gradients but lots of drama.

Monsal Head viaduct with the flat top of Fin Cop beyond

SHORT WALKS PEAK DISTRICT

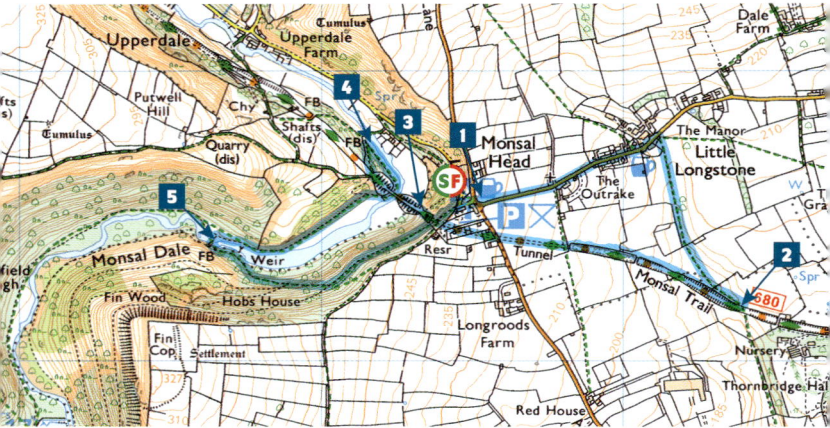

1 At the junction by the Monsal Head Hotel, cross the main road (B6465) and walk down the pavement of the lane into **Little Longstone**. About 100m beyond the Packhorse Inn cross over for the right hand of two footpaths across fields, keeping to the shallow valley bottom. Continue through gates to reach the **Monsal Trail**.

Inside Headstone Tunnel

WALK 4 – MONSAL HEAD TUNNEL AND VIADUCT

The viaduct seen from below

Since the trail is popular with cyclists as well as walkers, the etiquette for all users is to be considerate and alert, stay on the left and keep dogs under control. National Park advice is that making steam train noises is optional. Choo, choo!

2 Turn right and follow the trail for just over 1km, through the long curving Headstone Tunnel to emerge at the spectacular viaduct. It's advisable not to touch the sooty sides of the tunnel, as the black stains can be difficult to get out of skin and clothing.

3 Cross the viaduct and on the far side turn right through a gate, signposted Netherdale, for a stony path down to a path junction beside the **River Wye**.

4 Ignore the footbridge ahead and instead turn right along the bottom of **Monsal Dale**. Now go underneath the viaduct and out across open ground. Continue along this popular route past a **weir** until you reach a footbridge on the left.

Towering high above the wooded southern slopes of Monsal Dale is a flat-topped promontory known as Fin Cop. This was the site of a

SHORT WALKS PEAK DISTRICT

The Monsal Head Hotel

all the way to the top, from where there are stunning views down to the viaduct, finally emerging by the hotel and cafe at **Monsal Head**.

substantial hillfort constructed around 440BC and recent excavations have unearthed a mass burial site at the location.

Above the head of the dale was a farmhouse-turned-pub called the Bull's Head, but when the railway came along it was rebuilt and enlarged with a mock Alpine wooden frontage and renamed the Station Hotel. It's now called the Monsal Head Hotel and these days guests arrive with walking boots and bikes.

5 Cross the footbridge and follow the path left, now heading upstream past the weir. The path pulls away from the river and begins to gently rise through woodland. Ash dieback has affected many trees in Monsal Dale and a significant number have had to be felled and cleared. Follow the path

> **— To shorten**
>
> At Waypoint 4 cross the footbridge ahead, and behind the buildings turn right for a steep vehicle track back up to Monsal Head, which will give a walk of around 4km (1hr).

From awesome tunnel to mighty viaduct

Headstone Tunnel is the longest of the six tunnels on the Monsal Trail, at 487m, and since it gently curves you can't see the exit when you go in. Although the tunnel is open all the time it is only lit in daylight hours.

The five-arched Monsal Viaduct stands 230m above the River Wye and when you view it from below further on in the walk it's even more awe-inspiring! Trains first steamed across the viaduct in 1863; when the line closed a century later the Peak District National Park stepped in and the result is one of the most spectacular walking and cycling trails in England.

WALK 5
Sheldon and Magpie Mine

Start/finish	Main Street, Sheldon
Locate	///fountain.tidal.duck
Cafes/pubs	Pub in Sheldon
Transport	No public transport
Parking	Roadside on Main Street, Sheldon (DE45 1QS)
Toilets	No public toilets on route

Time 1¼hr
Distance 4.5km (2¾ miles)
Climb 55m

An easy ramble to explore the atmospheric remains of Magpie Mine and a remarkable Peak District industry

The limestone uplands of the White Peak were once the centre of the Britain's lead mining industry, and this easy walk along lanes and fields from the peaceful village of Sheldon visits the best-preserved site in the Peak District. Old buildings, chimneys, tunnels and spoil heaps reflect 300 years of effort as miners toiled to extract the valuable mineral, but the haunting remains also tell of the dangers and disappointments that went with it.

The Cornish engine house at Magpie Mine

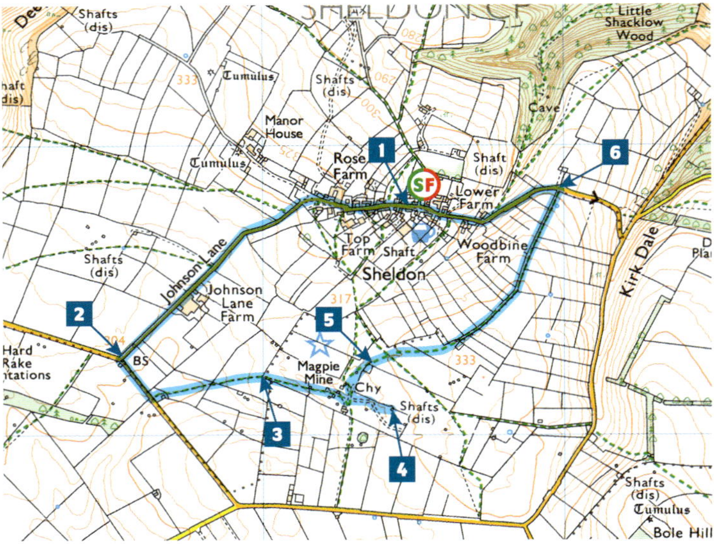

Sheldon's village pub, built from a former barn

1 From the pub walk up Main Street to the top of the village and stay on the lane as it swings left, past **Johnson Lane Farm**, and straight on across the open fields to a road junction at the end. A short walk to the east is Deep Dale Nature Reserve, a yellow carpet of cowslips every April and May.

2 At the junction turn left and in 100m go left over a stile for a field track past a dewpond. Follow the track as it begins to gently rise, then make for a wall stile visible on the skyline ahead.

Dewponds are small and shallow circular pools, traditionally lined

WALK 5 – SHELDON AND MAGPIE MINE

with clay, that were dug in fields to provide drinking water for livestock. They're a feature of limestone and chalk country, which holds little surface water, and are also valuable for wildlife.

3 Cross the stile and continue across bumpy ground to reach the cluster of mine buildings and old machinery. You can explore the whole site on foot, but this is a Scheduled Ancient Monument so be careful what you touch or disturb. Continue ahead to inspect a circular wooden contraption (a replica horse gin) on the far eastern edge of the site.

> Magpie Mine closed in the 1950s and was the last working mine in Derbyshire. The metal winding gear and cage date from then. If you look through the grille of the main shaft you may be able to see the water over 150m below. The Cornish engine house was built in 1868.

4 Go back to the tall circular chimney at the centre of the site and turn

Sheldon's main street, lined with huge mature trees

> ⓘ During the 17th and 18th centuries the White Peak was one of the most important lead mining areas in the world, with hundreds of active mines.

right to walk over to a circular stone hut. Continue past this then swing right and up to cross a wall stile and gate. The round stone hut is a former gunpowder store where explosives would be kept, deliberately away from the main buildings.

5 Follow the path across the middle of a field, with the horse gin over to your right. Go through another field and join a walled farm track and follow this all the way to where it ends at a road.

6 Turn left and follow the road back to the centre of **Sheldon**. The Cock and Pullet looks like a centuries-old village pub, but Sheldon's 'local' was in fact built in 1995 from a former barn.

Winding gear from the 1950s at Magpie Mine

The Peak District's mining heritage

Replica horse gin at Magpie Mine

For centuries men laboured underground at this site in an attempt to strike veins of precious lead ore. From a crude horse gin winching buckets of ore to the surface to more sophisticated pumping engines, it's a story of hard and dangerous work with no guarantee of success.

There's a permanent information point at the foot of the square tower, and Peak District Mines Historical Society, who look after the site, hold occasional heritage open days when guided tours are available (see https://pdmhs.co.uk/magpie-mine-peak-district). If you want to find out more visit the fascinating mining museum at Matlock Bath.

Sheepwash Bridge in Lathkill Dale

WALK 6
Monyash and upper Lathkill Dale

Start/finish	*Village green, Monyash*
Locate	*///pool.eternally.poetry*
Cafes/pubs	*Cafe and pub in Monyash*
Transport	*Buses from Bakewell*
Parking	*Car park on Chapel Street, Monyash (DE45 1JJ)*
Toilets	*On roadside at top of Lathkill Dale*

Time 2¼hr
Distance 6.5km (4 miles)
Climb 100m

An adventurous walk exploring the dramatic limestone geology of Lathkill Dale, with some rocky and uneven sections

The attractive White Peak village of Monyash sits at the head of Lathkill Dale, a narrow and steep-sided limestone valley characterised by caves, cliffs, screes and a disappearing river. This walk follows the valley-bottom path through the upper section, which in places is rocky underfoot and can be slippery after wet weather. It's a mini adventure and a hands-on geology lesson all in one, featuring one of the Peak District's most celebrated types of rock.

Upper Lathkill Dale

Upper Lathkill Dale can be a little rough underfoot

WALK 6 – MONYASH AND UPPER LATHKILL DALE

1 Walk east along Church Street past the church and village hall and out of the village along the wide verge. At a dip in the road turn right through a gate and along the broad grassy bottom of **Lathkill Dale** until you reach the second set of gates. This is one of five separate unspoilt limestone valleys that make up Derbyshire Dales National Nature Reserve (see Walk 3).

2 Go through the small gate directly ahead and take a path down the narrowing and initially leafy dale. Follow this rocky path between the boulders of former **Ricklow Quarry** then out along the open dale bottom. Go past **Lathkill Head Cave** and continue as far as Sheepwash Bridge (a wooden footbridge).

Jacob's ladder in Lathkill Dale

One of Lathkill Dale's most celebrated plants is Jacob's ladder, Derbyshire's county flower and nationally rare. In June and July look out for its purple-blue flowers and ladder-like leaves on the dale's open grassy slopes beyond Ricklow Quarry.

3 Cross the footbridge and take a narrow path up through patchy woodland. At a fork keep right on a rising path and

Bull's Head pub, Monyash

> ⓘ *The White Peak is dotted with traditional field barns that contained hay lofts above and cow stalls below, providing storage and shelter away from the farm.*

go up a short rocky staircase to reach the very top. Walk up through a small field to reach **One Ash Grange Farm**.

4 Follow the waymarked route through the farm and along a wide stony track past sheds. At the end go through the gate on the right, then immediately left, alongside a wall. Switch sides at the end of the field and carry on through several others until you reach a walled track. Follow this back to the road at **Monyash**.

5 Join the road at a bend then turn right along Church Lane. Across to the left is a natural pond called Fere Mere, the last survivor of five pools which once supplied the village with water. Continue through St Leonard's churchyard on a public footpath, then turn left onto Church Street to return to the village centre.

Two centuries ago Monyash had a thriving lead mining industry, and a special court, known as a Barmote Court, met at the Bull's Head pub on the green to settle disputes between miners.

— To shorten

For a gentler alternative to the rocky dale bottom, go through the gate on the right at Waypoint 2 and nearing One Ash Grange turn right to rejoin the main route back to Monyash, saving nearly 2km (around 1hr).

Limestone geology laid bare

Lathkill Head Cave in winter with the River Lathkill gushing out

Lathkill Dale is the result of water gradually eroding the Carboniferous limestone bedrock. It was laid down over 350 million years ago, with the pearly white rock exposed to form cliffs, crags and screes. Subsequently it has been used to build the drystone walls and field barns so characteristic of this area. Today, during winter, water usually gushes out of Lathkill Head Cave to form the River Lathkill. However, in the drier summer months the water table lowers and the river literally seeps away through the cracks in the porous limestone, abetted by old underground mineworkings, to leave the cave and riverbed dry. It creates what is sometimes called an ephemeral or winterbourne stream.

Well dressing takes place in Youlgrave each June

WALK 7
Lower Lathkill Dale and Bradford Dale

Start/finish	*Coldwell End car park, Youlgrave*
Locate	*///treble.trains.botanist*
Cafes/pubs	*Cafes and pubs in Youlgrave*
Transport	*Buses from Bakewell*
Parking	*Coldwell End car park (DE45 1WB)*
Toilets	*At Coldwell End car park*

Time 3hr
Distance 9.5km (6 miles)
Climb 155m

A long but scenic and straightforward walk through dales and over fields, celebrating local rivers and the role of water

Youlgrave (or Youlgreave) is flanked by two delectable dales with easy and attractive riverside routes. This walk links them both via gently rising field paths, including a short but steady woodland climb at the end. Rivers play an important part in the identity and heritage of White Peak villages like Youlgrave, where the supply of water is still celebrated in the local custom of well dressing.

Bridge in Bradford Dale between Alport and Youlgrave

SHORT WALKS PEAK DISTRICT

WALK 7 – LOWER LATHKILL DALE AND BRADFORD DALE

1 Turn right out of the car park and along the pavement, forking left at the turn for Middleton, then at the first bend go right up a gated path across a field to the road above. Cross this then follow the path directly opposite, up through more fields to a lane.

2 Cross the lane and continue through further fields and a woodland strip. Go over the next lane and head diagonally right on a well-walked route across three huge fields of open pasture, until you drop down to **Meadow Place Grange**. There are great views north to the outline of the Dark Peak, with the woods and moors of Chatsworth over to your right.

3 Walk straight ahead through the wide, gated farmyard, then cross to the far side of the next field for a gate in the right-hand corner. Follow the track down to cross the **River Lathkill** by a stone clapper bridge and turn right along the riverside path. Follow this popular route along the dale past pools until you reach **Conksbury Bridge**.

4 Turn right and cross the bridge. Follow the lane for 100m around bends and take a footpath on the left. Follow this for 1.3km through copses and fields, and across the end of a narrow lane, until you arrive at **Alport**.

Tree-lined pools in upper Bradford Dale

Just below the hamlet is an attractive and well-preserved corn mill dating from the 18th century.

5 Cross the road and join the path beside the **River Bradford**, which begins as a driveway next to the red telephone box (now housing a defibrillator). Continue along this wide track all the way upstream until you meet a road by the houses of **Youlgrave**.

Almost uniquely, Youlgrave has its own independent water company. Owned and run by the village, Youlgrave Waterworks Ltd has been supplying local households with drinking water since 1829.

6 Go over the road and through a gate to resume the riverside path past a small swimming pool created where the river has been dammed. At the end of the path turn left, cross a stone clapper bridge, then immediately go right to continue along the riverside path. Follow it into the wooded depths of Bradford Dale for 1km until you reach a wide stone bridge. Carved into the stonework of the bridge are lines from a Wordsworth poem, chosen by local people for a millennium arts project called Sites of Meaning.

7 Cross the bridge and as the path bends left and begins to steepen turn

Clapper bridge over the River Bradford at Youlgrave

A cold morning at the swimming pool in Bradford Dale

right. Follow this waterside path back down the dale (now on the opposite bank). The path then climbs steadily through woodland to reach the road at the top. Turn right to return to the car park at the start.

— To shorten

Just beyond Waypoint 6, before you reach the swimming area, follow a sloping tarmac path on the right up to the cafes and pubs in Youlgrave, with the car park at the far end of the main street. This will save about 1km (30min).

The art of well dressing

From May to September many White Peak villages put on well dressings, an ancient tradition that celebrates the local supply of fresh water. It involves pressing flower petals and a whole host of other natural materials like leaves, seeds and berries onto clay-lined boards to form intricate and colourful designs, usually depicting a story or a local theme. Youlgrave ritually 'dresses' five separate wells in mid to late June, which are then on display around the village for a week. To find out more, including dates of village well dressings, go to www.visitpeakdistrict.com/events/category/well-dressings.

Rocky pinnacle at Robin Hood's Stride

WALK 8
Elton and Robin Hood's Stride

Time 1½hr
Distance 5km (3 miles)
Climb 145m

An undulating ramble across farmland to visit an eye-catching rocky outcrop and an intriguing hermit's cave

Start/finish	Elton Church, Main Street, Elton
Locate	///soaps.hindering.pastime
Cafes/pubs	None on route
Transport	Buses from Bakewell and Matlock
Parking	Roadside on Main Street, Elton (DE4 2BZ)
Toilets	No public toilets on route

There's something irresistible about exploring the shapes, textures and hidden corners of a jumbled rocky outcrop, and so Robin Hood's Stride provides the perfect focus for this short and relatively easy walk from Elton. The lanes and field paths to get there and back are undulating but straightforward, while for added interest search out a genuine medieval hermit's cave in a nearby rockface.

The lane from Elton to Robin Hood's Stride

All Saints Church, Elton

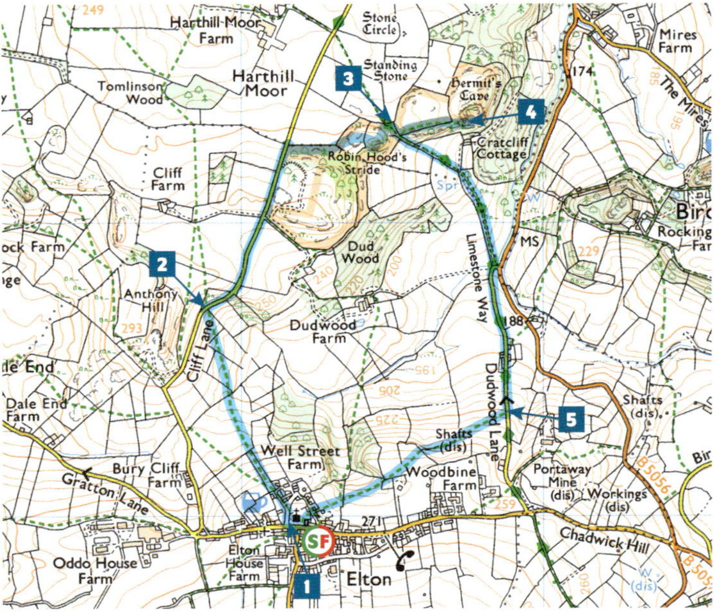

52

WALK 8 — ELTON AND ROBIN HOOD'S STRIDE

1 Walk down Well Street beside All Saints Church. The original medieval church had to be completely rebuilt after its steeple collapsed in 1805, weakened through subsidence caused by lead mining. Go left on the lower of two driveways and at a bend go left into a narrow field and onwards to a second. Turn sharply right and walk down the open slope beside the hedge (not the other route branching left). Follow it through scrubby fields and up to join a lane.

2 Turn right and walk along the road for 400m. Go right onto a path along the inside edge of a small wood, with open fields to the left, to reach **Robin Hood's Stride**. Robin Hood's Stride is also known as Mock Beggars Hall because of its outline. Walk in front of the rocks and down a tussocky slope to reach a small gate.

It's a fairly easy scramble up to the top of the rocks for superb views over the White Peak. Head to the right-hand side for a well-worn route up the back, but be careful of sudden and sheer drops.

3 Go through the small gate and a larger one just beyond. Walk ahead on an undulating grassy path and at the far side drop down to the right to cross a stile in the far bottom corner. Follow the path down through a jumble of rocks and tree roots to reach the **hermit's cave** beneath a sheer rock face on the left.

Robin Hood's Stride, also known as Mock Beggars Hall

Now protected by railings, the hermit's cave may date from as early as the 14th century and features an elaborate crucifix carved into the rockface, with a niche for a candle. Hermits often helped passing travellers, but the identity of this one is unknown.

4 Retrace your steps to the large gate at Waypoint 3 and turn left to walk down a track. At the very bottom don't join the main road on the left, but instead go straight on and walk up **Dudwood Lane** for 500m.

5 Turn right for a footpath that first crosses the open hillside and then climbs gently up the scrubby slope. During several snowy winters in the 1980s Elton villagers erected a temporary ski tow here, so they could

Hermit's cave near Robin Hood's Stride

WALK 8 – ELTON AND ROBIN HOOD'S STRIDE

Hermit's cave near Robin Hood's Stride

enjoy downhill skiing in Derbyshire. At the top, keep the playing field and pavilion over to your left and continue ahead via a stile, sharply down and then up the open field to reach **Elton** village. Follow the path between houses and through the churchyard to return to the start.

Robin Hood's giant stride

Robin Hood's Stride is a distinctive and eye-catching gritstone outcrop, so-called because the legendary outlaw is supposed to have leapt between the two main pinnacles or towers in one go. Its alternative name is Mock Beggars Hall, since from some angles its outline appears to resemble a long building with chimneys at either end. This intriguing jumble of rocks attracts a variety of visitors and you can spend plenty of time happily exploring its nooks and crannies. It's particularly popular with climbers, who come here to practise 'bouldering' or climbing without ropes on the rocks close to the ground.

Remains of a Saxon cross in Bakewell churchyard

WALK 9
Bakewell and the Monsal Trail

Start/finish	*Bakewell Visitor Centre, Bridge Street*
Locate	*///licks.miss.gent*
Cafes/pubs	*Wide choice in Bakewell, cafe at Hassop station*
Transport	*Buses from Derby, Sheffield and Buxton*
Parking	*Bakewell Bridge car park (DE45 1AQ)*
Toilets	*In Bakewell town centre (Granby Road)*

Time 1¾hr
Distance 6km (3¾ miles)
Climb 90m

Enjoy views over Bakewell's rooftops on this easy route taking in a former railway line

Although the last train may have departed years ago, Bakewell's railway line has been turned into a scenic traffic-free route for walkers and cyclists. This easy circuit above the town follows the Monsal Trail as far as the cafe at the former station at Hassop, returning on a wide and elevated track between fields with panoramic views across the rooftops and Wye valley.

On the easy descent to Bakewell

SHORT WALKS PEAK DISTRICT

WALK 9 – BAKEWELL AND THE MONSAL TRAIL

1 From **Bakewell Visitor Centre**, housed in the town's former market hall, walk along Bridge Street past the Queens Arms and over the road bridge. *Medieval in origin but widened since, this handsome structure has had to be periodically repaired after close brushes with today's unforgiving traffic.* Turn right and right again, into Coombs Road past the car park. After 300m turn left through gates on a public footpath up a driveway. This becomes a track along the right-hand side of a field until it reaches an old bridge at the very top.

2 Cross the bridge and go immediately left, through a gate, to drop down and join the **Monsal Trail**. Turn right and follow the former railway line past Bakewell station for just over 2km until you reach the next station at **Hassop**, now a cafe, gift shop and cycle hire centre.

> The former Midland Railway between London and Manchester closed in 1968, but although the signal boxes and goods yards have gone, many of the elegant Victorian station buildings remain intact and are now used as offices, shops and cafes.

Bakewell Bridge

SHORT WALKS PEAK DISTRICT

> ⓘ *The Monsal Trail is part of the 80km White Peak Loop, a walking and cycling circuit being developed to link Bakewell, Buxton and Matlock.*

3 From Hassop station continue along the trail for another 500m, then take a signposted public bridleway through a gate on the left. Follow this walled track up and across the gently undulating hillside with great views of Bakewell. Drop down the grassy hillside to join a wide track through woodland past **Holme Hall** and emerge on Holme Lane opposite a narrow stone bridge over the River Wye. This attractive five-arched Grade 1 listed packhorse bridge was built in 1684 and is one of the largely undiscovered gems of Bakewell.

4 Don't cross the packhorse bridge but turn left and walk along Holme Lane. Go through a gate into the second field on the right, called Wynn Meadow, and walk across to the River Wye. Stay on the riverside path through Scot's Garden all the way to the road bridge in **Bakewell**. Turn right across the bridge to return to the start.

The former Hassop station, now a cafe

WALK 9 – BAKEWELL AND THE MONSAL TRAIL

The famous Bakewell Pudding is not to be missed!

All Saints parish church dominates the town's southern aspect, as it has done for over a millennium. In the porch there is a display of ancient carved stones, while behind railings in the churchyard is the shaft of a Saxon cross dating from the early 9th century.

A short history of Bakewell

Bakewell's roots stretch back to Anglo-Saxon times when its natural springs and fording point over the River Wye attracted early setters. All Saints parish church, although rebuilt by the Normans, dates from this time and there was once a small castle to the east. Trading and latterly tourism has continued to make Bakewell a popular destination; its Monday street market has been going for over 600 years, while the livestock market is one of the last remaining in the region. Frequently bustling and sometimes quirky, Bakewell is a great base for exploring the Peak District. Visit the Old House Museum near the church to learn more about the town's interesting story.

Footpath beside the River Wye near Bakewell

WALK 10
Bakewell, Manners Wood and the River Wye

Start/finish	*Bakewell Visitor Centre, Bridge Street*
Locate	*///licks.miss.gent*
Cafes/pubs	*Wide choice in Bakewell*
Transport	*Buses from Derby, Sheffield and Buxton*
Parking	*Bakewell Bridge car park (DE45 1AQ)*
Toilets	*In Bakewell town centre (Granby Road)*

Time 2¾hr
Distance 9km (5½ miles)
Climb 165m

A moderately demanding walk exploring the richly wooded hills and riverside meadows surrounding the town

Situated deep in the Wye valley, Bakewell is ringed by hills and this walk begins with a long but steady climb up to the tree-covered slopes to the east. The path levels out and the mature, tranquil woodland is full of birds and wildflowers. An open and easy descent on tracks past Haddon Hall, with views across the valley, ends with a gentle return across tree-lined meadows beside the River Wye.

Bakewell Visitor Centre

SHORT WALKS PEAK DISTRICT

1 From **Bakewell Visitor Centre**, housed in the town's former market hall, walk along Bridge Street past the Queens Arms and turn right before the road bridge for the riverside path. Cross the footbridge, go over another and ahead towards the Agricultural Business Centre. Every Monday a vibrant and noisy livestock market takes place here, with cattle and sheep sold in large numbers. Go around the right-hand side of the main market building and on to reach **Coombs Road** at the far end.

2 Go half left across the road for a public footpath up a gated drive. Continue along the side of a field, over

the former railway, then carefully across a **golf course**, Walkers are requested to alert players to their presence by ringing the home-made bell provided. Still rising, the path enters woods, becomes rougher underfoot and beyond a small stream reaches a turning on the right.

Bakewell's weekly livestock market

> ⓘ *The unusually shaped roof of Bakewell Agricultural Business Centre is an acoustic ploy to muffle the sounds of animals in the livestock market.*

The mature woodland belt that extends along the hillside blends semi-natural and planted species, including larch, beech, oak and pine. From springtime bluebells to summer songbirds, it's a lovely nature walk that shouldn't be hurried.

3 Turn right, following Haddon Estate's waymarked Woodland Walk through **Manners Wood**. As the noticeboard explains, this is a concessionary path and very occasionally may be closed. Follow this wide, mostly level and delightful path through the trees for almost 3km. Where it eventually

SHORT WALKS PEAK DISTRICT

A quiet path in Manners Wood above Bakewell

> ⓘ In an average year around 200,000 sheep and 40,000 cattle and calves are sold at Bakewell's livestock market.

meets a wider path go ahead and downhill to reach a four-way junction of routes.

4 Go straight over on a wide farm track, fork right at the next junction and follow this all the way downhill. At the very bottom go right on a field path alongside railings above **Haddon Park** until you reach a driveway. Turn left and follow the surfaced lane downhill until just before the river crossing.

Among the trees in a cutting on the right is the closed-up tunnel of the former railway. The tunnel was insisted upon by the then Duke of Rutland so that the trains would remain out of sight and sound from his nearby family home.

5 Turn right through a gate and ahead on the path, taking the lower of two choices where it forks. A fenced-off and reclining veteran ash tree is

WALK 10 – BAKEWELL, MANNERS WOOD AND THE RIVER WYE

believed to be many hundreds of years old. Continue along the bank of the **River Wye**, or if the ground is flooded, simply switch to the higher route. Continue ahead across the meadows and alongside the open driveway to the Agricultural Business Centre. Retrace your steps to the start.

For much of this walk you are on land owned by Haddon Estate, which has been in the hands of the Manners family for generations. Their ancestral home is nearby Haddon Hall, a fortified medieval manor house that is open to the public.

– To shorten
At Waypoint 4 turn right along the wide vehicle track past Coombs Farm down to the end of Coombs Road and follow this (or the Monsal Trail above) back to Bakewell, saving around 800m (30min).

Veteran ash tree beside the River Wye

Grey's Tower, or the Reform Tower, on Stanton Moor

WALK 11
Stanton Moor

Start/finish	*Birchover Quarry public car park, Birchover Road*
Locate	*///starlight.broom.crop*
Cafes/pubs	*Pubs in Birchover*
Transport	*Buses from Bakewell and Matlock*
Parking	*Birchover Quarry public car park (DE4 2BN)*
Toilets	*No public toilets on route*

Time 1hr
Distance 4km (2½ miles)
Climb 50m

This easy circuit of diminutive Stanton Moor reveals some intriguing historical remains, including an ancient stone circle

This patch of attractive heather moor and birch woodland between Bakewell and Matlock may not be very big, but views from the elevated position are superb. Closer to hand there's evidence of long-established settlement, with ancient cairns, tumuli and a Neolithic stone circle, not to mention some weirdly sculpted rocks. It's a short and very easy outing that mostly sticks to well-walked paths and sandy tracks.

Stanton Moor

1 Leave the lower end of the car park opposite **Birchover Quarry** and take a gated path that swings round to the road. Turn left and immediately right at the junction and go along the lane for 400m. Birchover Quarry produces a popular architectural gritstone, warm and light pink in colour, used most notably as external cladding on Portcullis House in London.

2 Go over a stile on the left for a broad path up onto **Stanton Moor**. Turn right at a junction of paths, then when you come to a stile in the fence on the right cross this and turn left. Now walk along the edge of the moor, with great views across the Derwent valley to Matlock, until you reach a tall stone tower.

The slender gritstone structure is known as Grey's Tower or the Reform Tower. It was built in 1832 by the local landowner to commemorate the passing of the Reform Act, a major electoral change championed by Whig prime minister Earl Grey.

3 Go over the stile in the fence directly behind the tower and turn right on the path. Follow this until you reach **Nine Ladies stone circle**. There are other stone circles and dozens of Bronze Age cairns and burial mounds scattered across the moorland.

4 Walk straight ahead through the circle and past the isolated **King Stone**. Continue on a clear path

Stanton Moor provides easy walking

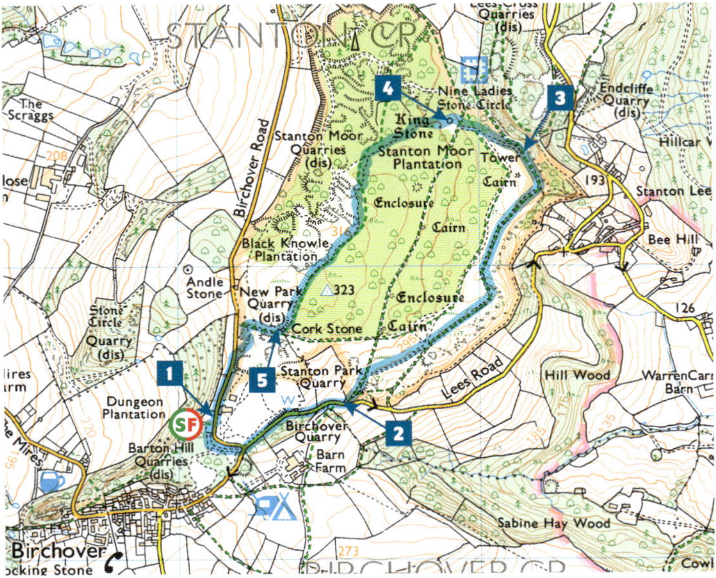

The Cork Stone

through the bracken and silver birch woodland, swinging left by the corner of a fence. Fork left by a fallen tree and out across the open moor past small and long disused quarries on a clear path.

5 When you reach the **Cork Stone** turn right and down to a gate. Beyond this turn left for a shortcut to the road. Turn left along the road to return to the start. Next to Birchover village are Rowtor Rocks, with odd carvings, steps and caves, where a 17th-century local rector once dabbled in witchcraft.

The Cork Stone is an enormous block of weathered sandstone that perches in isolation on the moor. It's named after its unusual shape, and metal handholds mean that it's possible for agile visitors to climb to the very top.

+ To lengthen

From the back of the car park at the start, a public footpath slopes down through the trees, emerging eventually at the end of Birchover's main street, opposite the Druid Inn, a round trip of 700m (30min).

Nine Ladies stone circle

Nine Ladies stone circle

As with so many ancient sites, it's unclear whether the 4000-year-old Nine Ladies stone circle was built for ceremonial burials, as a trading point or simply just somewhere to meet. According to popular folklore, it takes its name from a group of women who were turned to stone for dancing on a Sunday; and the so-called King Stone nearby is said to be the fiddler. It's usually a very quiet place, but be aware that each year Nine Ladies stone circle attracts large crowds of people celebrating the summer solstice, so if you want a peaceful walk it's best to avoid a few days in mid-June!

Gentle riverside walking through Chatsworth Park

WALK 12
Chatsworth Park and Edensor

Start/finish	Calton Lees, Chatsworth
Locate	///grapevine.overruns.resolves
Cafes/pubs	Tea room at Edensor, cafe and kiosk at Chatsworth House
Transport	Buses from Sheffield and Bakewell
	Parking Calton Lees car park (DE4 2NX)
Toilets	Outside main entrance of Chatsworth House (10min off route)

Time 2hr
Distance 6.5km (4 miles)
Climb 145m

A gentle tour of Chatsworth's landscaped parkland and estate village, taking in views of the impressive stately home itself

No visit to the Peak District is complete without a walk around Chatsworth, whose extensive landscaped grounds are free to explore on foot. This route climbs gently to the western edge of the park, from where there are spectacular views, then via the unusual estate village of Edensor down to the stately pile beside the river. If you want to explore the house and gardens (there's an entrance fee, but it's worth it), then factor in plenty of extra time or plan a separate visit.

Chatsworth House, seat of the Duke of Devonshire

SHORT WALKS PEAK DISTRICT

1 From the car park at **Calton Lees** walk along the lane past the entrance to the garden centre. At a junction, where the lane bends left, go straight over and take a gated vehicle track along the bottom of the gently rising valley. Continue up past **Calton Houses** until you reach a path junction beyond a gate.

2 Go right and across the open hill-top of Calton Pastures, aiming to the left of an open barn in front of woodland ahead. Take a gated track through the trees and enter **Chatsworth Park**.

The open parkland leads down to the River Derwent, on the far side of which is Chatsworth House, which

WALK 12 — CHATSWORTH PARK AND EDENSOR

The estate village of Edensor

now gleams after its limestone exterior was restored a few years ago. On the wooded hilltop above is the 16th-century Hunting Tower.

3 Walk down the open slope ahead, with the House over to your right. Keep to the left of a small evergreen plantation and then head in the direction of the church spire of **Edensor**. Take a gated and stepped path, just to the left of the church. At the bottom turn right and walk through the village on the road to reach the main vehicle entrance.

Edensor churchyard contains the grave of Kathleen Kennedy who married the elder son of the 10th Duke of Devonshire in 1944. She died in a plane crash four years later and in 1963 her grave was visited by her brother, President John F. Kennedy.

4 Leave the estate village by the pedestrian gate next to the cattle grid. Almost every building in Edensor is in a different style, supposedly because the 6th Duke couldn't make

Chatsworth Bridge

77

The River Derwent running through Chatsworth Park

up his mind what he wanted! Cross the road and follow the popular path straight ahead, which leads to the bridge in front of the magnificent **Chatsworth House**.

5 Go right before the bridge and walk along the broad grassy bank of the **River Derwent** opposite the House. Just before you reach the remains of old mill buildings, veer right up to the road and cross this to return to the car park at the start. The former corn mill was partly destroyed when three huge beech trees fell on it in a great gale in 1962.

> **+ To lengthen**
>
> At Waypoint 5 cross the bridge for the short walk up to Chatsworth House where there's a cafe and toilets outside that you can use without paying to enter, a round trip of 600m or 20min.

Exploring Chatsworth on foot

Chatsworth has been the seat of 17 generations of the Devonshire family across five centuries and is one of the premiere stately homes in England. As well as the magnificent mansion, with its valuable art collection, there's an extensive garden, farm shop and other visitor attractions. The River Derwent runs through the heart of the elegant parkland, which is home to a free-roaming herd of fallow deer and surrounded by a 15km-long drystone wall and deer fence. Most of Chatsworth Park is open to walkers and is a great place for a leisurely roam and a picnic on a warm summer's day.

WALK 13
Beeley and Hob Hurst's House

Start/finish	Devonshire Square, Beeley
Locate	///safely.microchip.mankind
Cafes/pubs	Cafe and pub at Beeley
Transport	Buses from Matlock
Parking	Roadside on Devonshire Square, Beeley (DE4 2NZ)
Toilets	No public toilets on route

Time 2½hr
Distance 8km (5 miles)
Climb 230m

An energetic walk on sometimes rough paths up to the high moors above Chatsworth to visit a prehistoric burial mound

From the peaceful former estate village of Beeley the route climbs steadily via a small plantation and out across the open moorland on unmade paths, which may be boggy in places. At the very top, from where the views are fantastic, is a small prehistoric burial mound known as Hob Hurst's House, named after a local goblin. Then it's a gradual descent to Beeley on moorland tracks and field paths with more sweeping views of the Derwent valley.

The Old Smithy tea rooms at Beeley

SHORT WALKS PEAK DISTRICT

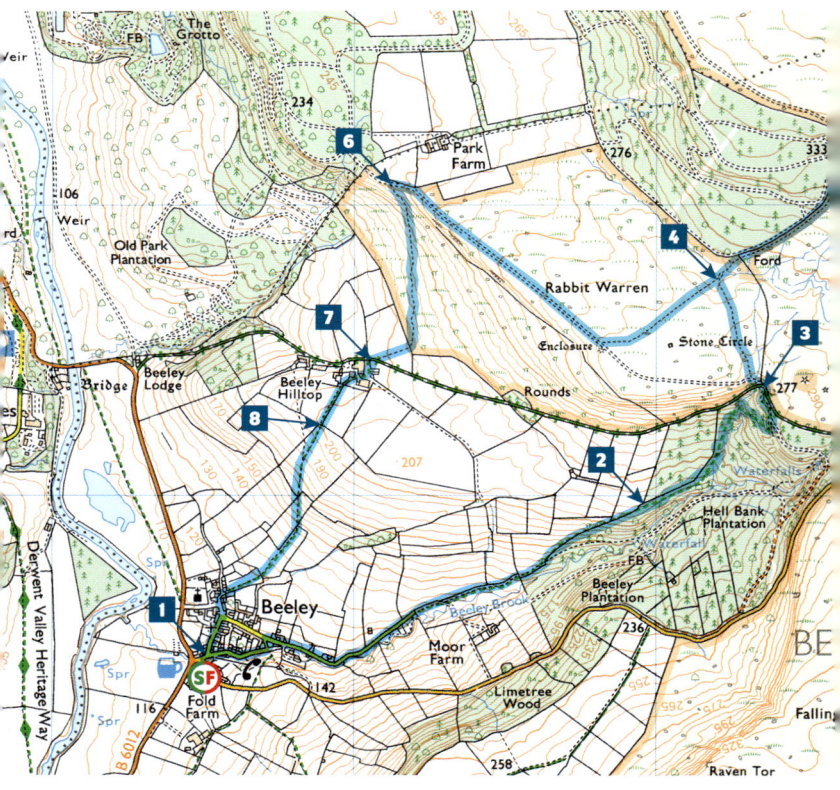

1 Facing the front door of the pub, go left along the lane beside **Beeley Brook**. King Edward VII visited the Devonshire Arms on several occasions and it's rumoured he met his mistress Alice Keppel here. At the end follow it round to the left and then turn right at the junction to walk along a lane. When the tarmac drive bears right go straight on uphill along a rough track. Go through one gate, ignore a second on the right, and through another to enter woodland.

2 Stay on the main path, which soon winds its way left and uphill through the sometimes dense **Hell Bank Plantation**. At the head of the narrow

WALK 13 – BEELEY AND HOB HURST'S HOUSE

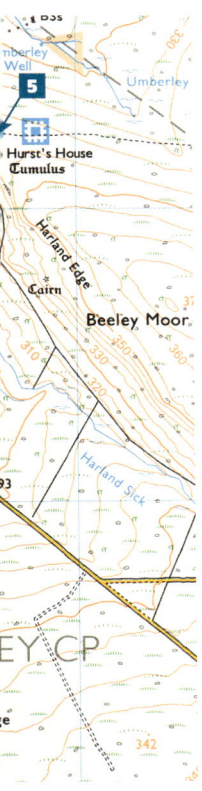

Beeley's colourful gardens

valley cross a small bridge and keep right on a gently rising path. Turn sharply left at a junction by a waymark post and follow this path along the top of the woods and out to an unmade lane. The woods and moors above Beeley are peaceful now, but once there were coal pits, lead smelting mills and quarries producing gritstone for buildings like Chatsworth.

3 Go straight across the lane to a high stepped wall stile opposite and in 50m turn right on a small path signposted Hob Hurst's House. Follow this waymarked route across the open moorland until you reach a small bridge.

4 Go across the bridge and keep ahead on the walked path, close to a wall on your left, up to the skyline and a junction of paths. **Hob Hurst's House** is a short distance to your right on the end of Harland Edge.

> There isn't much left of Hob Hurst's House these days. The small rectangular mound has an outer ditch and bank and it may have been used as a burial site in Bronze or Iron Age times. But the view from this house is five star!

A wall stile onto the moor

5 Return along the same route and beyond the bridge at Waypoint 4 fork

The heather-covered mound of Hob Hurst's House

Moorland above Beeley

right and at the end turn right to follow a broad track across the moors.

> An extensive strip of heather moorland borders the Derwent valley at this point, including East Moor and Beeley Moor, and for a short period around mid-August it turns a bright and vivid purple when the heather is in bloom.

6 Just before you reach the woods, near **Park Farm**, head sharply left and down a narrow sloping path through a young plantation and then out across a field to reach a lane.

7 Go right for a few paces then immediately left on a waymarked path across the farmyard of **Beeley Hilltop**. Walk along the farm track beside a wall until you enter a field at the top of an open slope, with the village below.

8 Go straight ahead down the sloping pasture, swinging right in the third field to emerge in **Beeley** village. Turn left then fork right at the junction to return to the start. Beeley's unspoilt charm is partly due to the fact that for several centuries much of it was owned by Chatsworth, whose workers lived in rented cottages.

Looking south from Curbar Edge to Baslow Edge

WALK 14
Baslow Edge and Curbar Edge

Start/finish	*Curbar Gap car park*
Locate	*///windows.fountain.precluded*
Cafes/pubs	*Pub in Curbar and cafe in Calver*
Transport	*No public transport*
Parking	*Curbar Gap car park, Clodhall Lane (S32 3YR)*
Toilets	*No public toilets on route*

Time 2¼hr
Distance 7km (4¼ miles)
Climb 110m

Airy tracks high above the Derwent valley provide sensational views, with a return across rougher moorland paths

The Derwent valley defines the eastern edge of the Peak District and is lined by a high and almost continuous rocky edge, with moorland behind stretching towards Chesterfield and Sheffield. This walk takes you from one breathtaking edge-top viewpoint to another, linked by a path across bare moorland which after wet weather may be boggy in places. Also be careful of sheer drops on the unfenced edges.

Wellington's Monument

SHORT WALKS PEAK DISTRICT

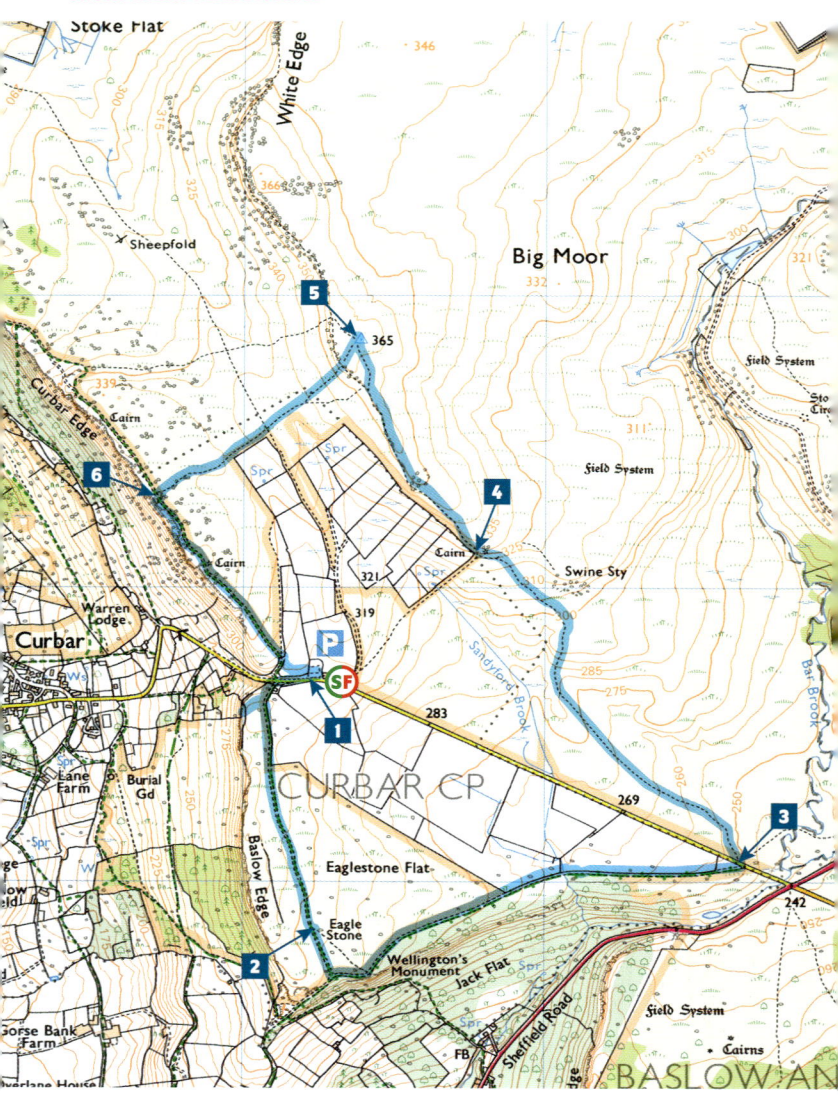

WALK 14 — BASLOW EDGE AND CURBAR EDGE

1 From the car park entrance turn right onto the road and then left onto the wide track along **Baslow Edge**. The route doesn't follow the actual outer edge, but after a few paces a short there-and-back path on the right leads to a popular viewpoint. Continue all the way along the main track until you reach a large gritstone rock called the **Eagle Stone**.

> According to local custom, before the young men of Baslow could marry they first had to prove themselves by climbing to the top of the Eagle Stone.

2 Continue along the route until you reach a junction at the end, with views of distant Chatsworth straight ahead. Turn left to walk past **Wellington's Monument** and all the way along the wide track until you reach a road. Wellington's Monument commemorates the Duke's victory at Waterloo in 1815 and complements a memorial to Admiral Nelson on nearby Birchen Edge.

3 Cross the road, go through the gate on the far side and out onto open moorland. The path heads half left and maintains its direction over rough and bumpy ground. Make for the high point on the skyline ahead, gradually rising and forking right at the foot of a sharper slope. After 1.5km you reach a signpost near the corner of a wall.

The Eagle Stone with the moor's resident herd of Highland cows

An old guidestone, or stoop, for early travellers

At the far northern end of the ridge is White Edge Lodge, a strikingly isolated and remote cottage that was used in the 2011 film adaptation of *Jane Eyre*. It is now rented out by the National Trust for visitor accommodation.

5 Ignore the path straight ahead, beyond the trig point, and instead turn left on a narrower path. Go across the main path to White Edge and continue directly ahead, down the slope and then alongside a wall, until you reach **Curbar Edge**.

4 Go straight on, signposted **White Edge**, and as you approach the top fork right to reach the white-painted trig point.

6 Turn left onto the broad and popular route just back from the edge.

Open moorland above Curbar

Beyond a gate go left on a path signposted White Edge to reach the car park. The road through Curbar Gap was once a packhorse route and later a turnpike, when users would have to pay a toll for its upkeep.

> **— To shorten**
>
> At Waypoint 4 turn left for a well-walked path, signposted Curbar, straight back to the car park at the start, saving 2km (around 45min).

Wildlife of the Eastern Moors

The Eastern Moors includes not just rough grassland but bog, heath and woodland, and this mix of habitat supports a range of wildlife. Owls, golden plovers and curlews all make their home here, while skylarks can often be heard (if not seen) trilling high overhead. On warm and sunny days look down at your feet to glimpse the dark stripes of an adder before it slithers away; while in autumn listen for the bellows and barks of rutting red deer, as Britain's largest native mammal begins its annual courtship ritual.

The high arched bridge at Froggatt

WALK 15
River Derwent and Calver Weir

Start/finish	*Calver Bridge*
Locate	*///sizzled.pills.propelled*
Cafes/pubs	*Cafe and pub by Calver Bridge*
Transport	*Buses from Sheffield*
Parking	*On roadside at Calver Bridge*
Toilets	*No public toilets on route*

Time 1¼hr
Distance 4.5km (2¾ miles)
Climb 20m

An easy figure-of-eight wander along the tree-lined River Derwent via a historic weir

This is a relaxing riverside walk through the trees beside the wide and fast-flowing Derwent, taking in handsome stone bridges and an equally historic weir across the river. It's a flat and easy route, although the woodland paths can be muddy after rain and care is needed crossing the main road at New Bridge halfway round.

The tree-lined River Derwent

Stocking Farm was once used as a Sunday School

1 Facing the front door of the Bridge Inn, turn right and walk across the old road bridge (there's a modern one nearby). Locally Calver is pronounced 'carver' and appears to merge with Curbar at the start. Turn right by Calver Mill Gallery, then follow the surfaced drive past **Stocking Farm** and out across an open field. Stocking Farm has an unusual building with a bell tower which was built in 1817 as a Sunday school for the mill workers' children. Join the broad track beyond, alongside an old drainage channel known as The Goit, all the way to **New Bridge**.

2 Cross the A625 carefully on the tight bend, but don't go over the bridge itself. Look for the gate and squeeze stile in the wall opposite and take the clear path beyond. Follow this riverside route upstream, forking right over a small footbridge, until after just over 1km you reach the bridge at **Froggatt**.

Rather confusingly, there are four rivers in England called the Derwent. Derbyshire's version rises on the boggy slopes of Bleaklow, high up in the Dark Peak, then flows south for 80km via Matlock and Derby to join the River Trent.

3 Cross the handsome and high-arched bridge and on the far side turn right along the lane. After 75m go right again to resume the riverside path beside the **River Derwent**, now heading downstream. Just before you reach New Bridge go left on a ramped path up to the road.

Despite its name, New Bridge was built in 1781 and is one of the main routes from Sheffield into the Peak District. Further upstream, Froggatt bridge had to be extended with an extra arch when the construction of Calver Weir caused the river to widen.

4 Cross the road and go down steps to carry on along the broad riverbank track until you reach **Calver Weir**.

If you look across the curving weir you'll see that the smoothly

WALK 15 – RIVER DERWENT AND CALVER WEIR

sloping barrier incorporates what looks like a narrow walled channel. This is a fish pass that allows safe passage for fish like brown trout and grayling, which spawn upstream.

5 Continue along the path until you reach a road, opposite the former Calver Mill. Calver Mill was used to depict Colditz Castle in the 1970s TV series about prisoners of war (it's now private apartments). Turn right to return to the start.

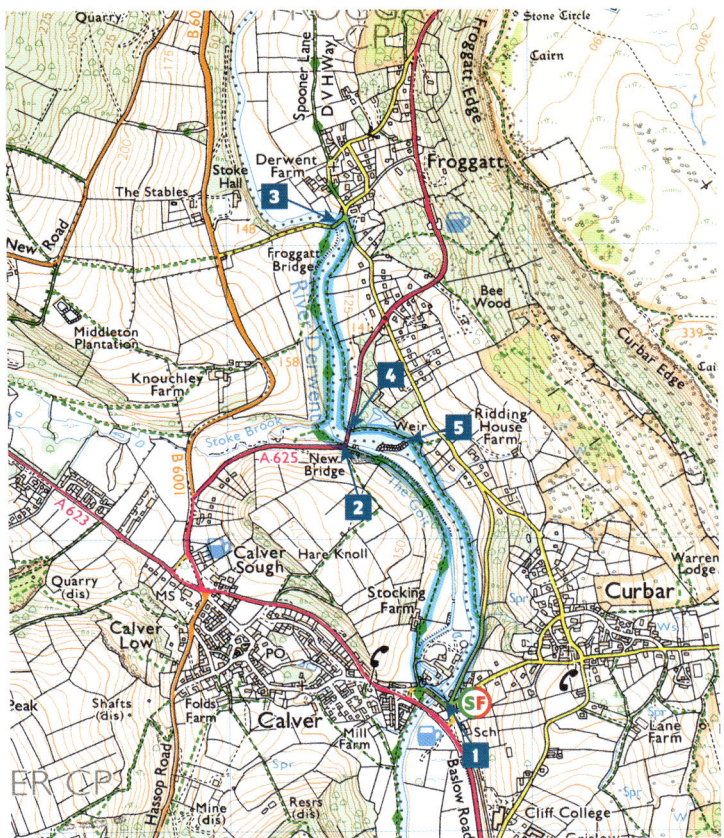

Calver Weir

> ### − To shorten
> At Waypoint 2 go across New Bridge and turn right for the path back along the far bank, omitting the second loop of the walk and saving just over 1.5km (30min).

Calver Weir

A weir is simply a dam or barrier built across a river to alter the flow or raise the river level. Calver Weir was built in the 1840s to hold back and channel water to the cotton mill at nearby Calver, where it powered the machinery. The weir is 106m long and built in a reverse 'S' shape in order to relieve what can be the considerable pressure of the river in full flow (a previous weir was washed away). After years of neglect and to save it from potential collapse, the scheduled monument was restored in 2010 at a cost of £1.8 million.

USEFUL INFORMATION

Tourism bodies

Visit Peak District & Derbyshire www.visitpeakdistrict.com

Peak District National Park www.peakdistrict.gov.uk

The National Trust www.nationaltrust.org.uk

Eastern Moors www.visit-eastern-moors.org.uk

Chatsworth www.chatsworth.org

Haddon www.haddonhall.co.uk

Tourist information centres

Old Market Hall, Bridge Street, Bakewell,
www.peakdistrict.gov.uk/visiting/visitor-centres/bakewell

Buses

Buses to Bakewell from Matlock, Chesterfield, Sheffield and local village services
www.hulleys-of-baslow.co.uk

Bus to Bakewell from Matlock and Derby
www.trentbarton.co.uk

Bus to Bakewell and Chatsworth from Sheffield
www.tmtravel.co.uk

Bus to Bakewell from Matlock and Buxton
www.highpeakbuses.com

Bus from Buxton to Sheffield via Tideswell and open-top Peak Sightseer (seasonal)
www.stagecoachbus.com

© Andrew McCloy 2025
First edition 2025
ISBN: 978 1 78631 257 0
eISBN: 978 1 78765 190 6

Printed in Singapore by KHL Printing on responsibly sourced paper.
A catalogue record for this book is available from the British Library.
All photographs are by the author unless otherwise stated.
Cover illustration of the Monsal Head Viaduct by Avery Mitchell.

© Crown copyright and database rights 2025 OS AC0000810376

Cicerone's EU representative for GPSR compliance is Easy Access System Europe, Mustamäe tee 50, 10621 Tallinn, Estonia. Email gpsr.requests@easproject.com.

CICERONE

Cicerone Press, Juniper House, Murley Moss, Oxenholme Road,
Kendal, Cumbria, LA9 7RL

www.cicerone.co.uk

Updates to this Guide

While every effort is made to ensure the accuracy of guidebooks as they go to print, changes can occur during the lifetime of an edition. Any updates that we know of for this guide will be on the Cicerone website (www.cicerone.co.uk/1257/updates), so please check before planning your trip. We also advise that you check information about transport, accommodation and shops locally. Even rights of way can be altered over time. We are always grateful for information about any discrepancies between a guidebook and the facts on the ground, sent by email to updates@cicerone.co.uk.

Register your book: To sign up to receive free updates, special offers and GPX files where available, create a Cicerone account and register your purchase via the 'My Account' tab at www.cicerone.co.uk.